The 23rd Psalm

T Lee Sizemore

This is a work of non-fiction.
Text and Illustrations copyrighted
by T Lee Sizemore, DVM, RN ©2017

All rights reserved.
No part of this book may be
reproduced, transmitted,
or stored in an information retrieval
system in any form or by any means,
graphic, electronic, or
mechanical without prior written
permission from the author.
LCCN: 2017918462
First Edition 2017

Printed in the United States of America
A 2 Z Press LLC
PO Box 582
Deleon Springs, FL 32130
bestlittleonlinebookstore.com
bestlittleonlinebookstore@gmail.com
386-681-7402
ISBN: 978-1-946908-96-4

Dedication

This book is dedicated in
memory of my
beloved grandfather,
Alexander Balcziunas

Psalm 23

The Lord is my Shepherd,
I shall not lack,
He makes me lie down
in green pastures,
He leads me beside still waters,
He restores my soul.
Yes, though I walk
through the valley of the
shadow of death,
I will fear no evil,
for Your rod and Your staff comfort me.
You prepare a table for me
in the presence of my enemies,
You anoint my head with oil,
my cup runs over.
Surely goodness and mercy will follow me
All the days of my life,
and I will dwell in the house
of the Lord forever.

...so I give

all my cares to

Him.....

...so I can exerience His peace and the assurance of His love...

He leads me
in the path
of righteousness
for His
name's sake....
Psalm 23.3b

Yeah,
tho I walk
through
the valley
of the
shadow of
death.....
Psalm 23.4a

For Your are with me,
Your rod and Your
staff comfort me...
Psalm 23.4c

...the beautiful anointing of the power of God...

...the goodness and mercy that comes from You, my Abba Father.....

...and I
will dwell in the
house of the
Lord forever....
Psalm 23.6b

AMEN

ABOUT THE AUTHOR

T Lee Sizemore has cherished
her faith for many years.
She loves the Bible
and all it has taught her about
the God she loves.
Psalm 23 is meaningful to her life
as she is certain it is to others'.
The author hopes everyone enjoys
this little book as
much as she enjoyed writing it.

Other Books by T Lee Sizemore

D is for Dog-
An Easy Guide to
Veterinary Care for Dogs

C is for Cat-
An Easy Guide to
Veterinary Care for Cats

H is for Horse- An
Easy Guide to
Veterinary Care for Horses

A Few Short Stories-
Stories to Inspire Writing Topics

There's Always Hope

The Magic of Christmas

Coming Soon Titles
By T Lee Sizemore

R is for Rabbit-

An Easy Guide to

Veterinary Care for Rabbits

P is for Pocket Pets-

An Easy Guide to Veterinary

Care for Pocket Pets-

Hamsters, Gerbils, Mice

F is for Ferret-

An Easy Guide to

Veterinary Care for Ferrets

S is for Sheep-

An Easy Guide to

Veterinary Care for Sheep

Also coming are:

Divine Designs- A Children's Book

The Amazing Body Series –

Easy Guides to Anatomy and Physiology

for the Human Body

The Mailbox- A Fiction Title

A 2 Z Press LLC

A 2 Z Press LLC
is a publishing company created by
T Lee Sizemore for the purpose of
publishing literary works
by new and aspiring writers.
All content is G- rated
and we welcome your submissions
of ideas for children's literature as well as
young adult and self – help topics.
Science and medicine,
holidays and other interesting
topics are all welcome.

Submit queries to
bestlittleonlinebookstore@gmail.com
Or to PO Box 582 Deleon Springs, FL 32130

Visit our Website –

At bestlittleonlinebookstore.com
for blogs, book sales, quilt
and craft sales, gifts,
low cost original card
sales and more!

Dedication

The Author
would like to include an
additional dedication
of this book to the
loving memory
of her beloved brother,
David Sizemore,
who went home to be with the
Lord June 27, 2017

He knows

the Lord is his Shepherd.

www.ingramcontent.com/pod-product-compliance
Lightning Source LLC
Chambersburg PA
CBHW041959080526
44588CB00021B/2811